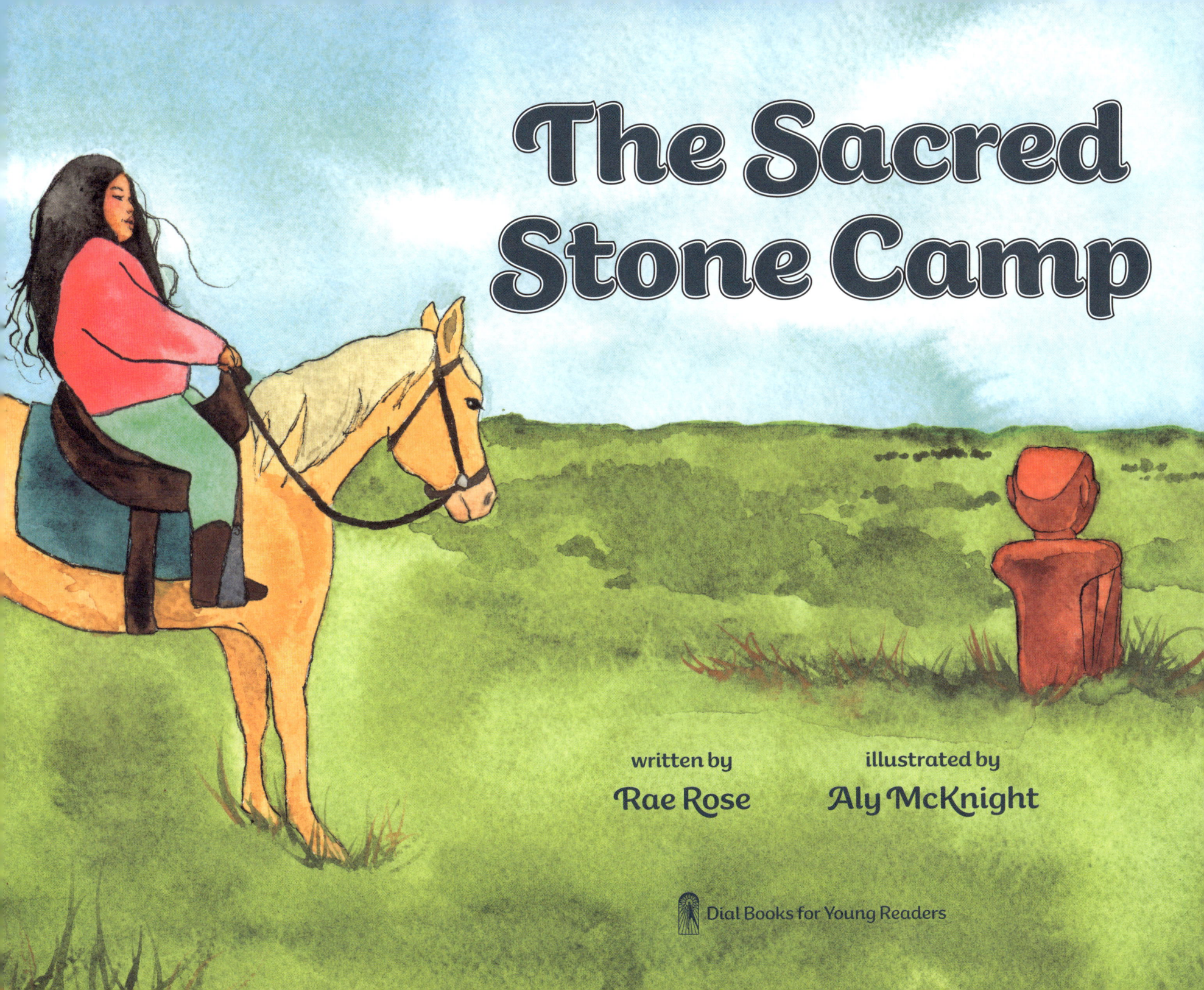

The Sacred Stone Camp

written by
Rae Rose

illustrated by
Aly McKnight

Dial Books for Young Readers

The land is sacred to the people. The people are sacred to the land.

Snowflakes dance and flutter softly through the air.
Musty paws the hard, cold earth.

Our breath combines, forming soft clouds rising like a prayer.
Standing here with Musty, I wait for Lala Miles and Unci
LaDonna to return with their own horses and Musty's saddle.

Everyone surrounding me is strong; their hope and excitement fill the air like electricity. A coffee can to smudge is brought around. An elder's words have been spoken and the songs have begun. Musty neighs, shaking out her freshly brushed mane.

Opening the Sacred Stone Camp is an important step in stopping DAPL's Black Snake from destroying our water and land. I want to be brave and strong like all of them, but I have my secret fears. If I am honest, I feel uneasy against a threat so big. Icy knots form, falling uncomfortably in the pit of my belly as I think of the Black Snake's attack.

As if by magic, as if they heard my secret worries rattling around in my head, I feel Unci's warmth as her arms pull me in. Just like that, all my doubts quiet. "Lil' Donna, are you okay?" Unci LaDonna asks. Lala Miles is there too, Musty's saddle in hand.

"I was just thinking about the stand we are making and all the things that could go wrong if we don't win," I admit.

"That is a lot for one protector to think about." Unci hugs me tight. "Most important to remember is that we stand together, always. Look at all the people here today. We are all here to support each other as we stand up to protect Unci Maka. We will always be stronger when we come together to support one another."

I nod. I know she is right. Even if we fail, we have to try to protect the lands and waters we love and need.

"My girl, we will always be here to help you," Lala Miles assures me. "Now show me your brave and beautiful smile." He smiles too as he helps me up into Musty's saddle. Lala carefully adjusts the stirrups to my new height.

"I'm ready." This time, I really feel ready, excitement replacing the fear. After all, I have my unci and lala beside me.

Finally, we are all ready to go. Those who can have mounted their horses, and the elders and small children are packed into vehicles to follow behind. We are all ready to defend the water and protect the land against DAPL's Black Snake.

"Hoka!" Lala Miles calls, pulling me out of my thoughts. Lala is ready to lead us forward.

Unci LaDonna winks as she motions me to the front. My heart warms as I take my place beside Unci and Lala to lead everyone to where, from today on, the Sacred Stone Camp will begin.

Those on horseback release their reins as our eager steeds trot forward, their heads held high as they neigh to our songs and the strength of our battle cries.

As we fall into a steady pace, I ask, "Unci, tell me again why you named the camp Sacred Stone?"

I love to hear Unci's stories about the land.

Unci LaDonna smiles. "Long before you were born the Cannonball River and the Missouri River came together in a magical way, forming perfect circular rocks. Those rocks looked like cannonballs; that is where the Cannonball River got her name.

"Because of the dam, the two rivers can no longer meet in that sacred way, but I wanted to name this camp after those sacred stones. I want everyone to remember the beautiful way those rivers came together before they were stolen away by the dam."

I can see the sacred stones forming as Unci speaks. With every word, the great rivers and stones come to life once again in my mind.

As we ride along Unci LaDonna points out her memories with other sacred stones across these hills and prairies. I look out at the light snow dusting the land as I listen to Unci's voice. My own experiences from today will form into beautiful memories of my own. Memories of this very special moment, on this very precious day, surrounded by my unci's and lala's love.

Unci LaDonna and Lala Miles have told me stories about Lakota dreamers who have brought important prophecies back to the people.

Some of these dreams warned us about the Black Snakes. We were told that these Black Snakes would ravage the land and poison the waters. We have seen the oil spills, the loss of habitat, and the sickness from toxic waste. The more the Black Snakes encroach, the more the land and water die.

Greed brought the Black Snakes to life. We are here because we hope love can stop the Black Snakes' destruction. I know that we can create a different future. A future where our good intentions lead to actions that will heal Ina Maka, keeping her vibrant and strong. That is the future my family is fighting for.

The Black Snakes have been attacking other tribes for longer than I have been alive. My family has been trying to stop this sneaky DAPL Black Snake for a very long time too. If this Black Snake is not stopped, it will poison the Cannonball, Missouri, and Mississippi rivers that millions of people depend on.

We can live without the Black Snake's oil, but we cannot live without Unci Maka's precious lands and waters.

Unci LaDonna calls out for my attention, pointing to a special site. A perfectly round stone stands on a pillar all alone. A memory of two rivers who met in a sacred way, not so long ago.

Excited, I yell out, "A Sacred Stone!"

"We are almost there." Lala Miles smiles as he leads us off the main road and onto a dirt path that Lala calls a reservation road.

Riding down the slope, we sing and holler our way into the first day of the Sacred Stone Camp. I have never seen this land look so small, but with every vehicle, horse, and person, the Sacred Stone lands fill to the brim with love.

After Musty and her fellow horses are cared for, we are ready for the real work to begin. I feel a strong pride looking at everyone arriving here, and it makes me feel taller, my first steps forward feel stronger.

Unci LaDonna, Lala Miles, and the other adults have so much work to do. They are busy setting up the tipis and other structures that the Water Protectors will need to live here. The other kids and I want to help too. So together we form our own plan of action.

We set up a delivery system to relay messages and deliver items. We make sure the elders are comfortable and watch the smaller kids while the adults work the day away.

It feels like mere moments before the soft hue of evening paints the land. There's a chill in the air even before I see the Firekeepers getting ready to start the Sacred Stone's first flame.

Excited, I yell to the kids I have been playing hide-and-seek with. "Come out, come out, wherever you are. It is time to light the fire!" All the kids start popping out and we head back to our adults hand in hand.

Running to Unci, I ask, "Are you done with all the work?"

"No, little one, there is still a lot of work to do, but we have done all the work we can today. The horses have been loaded up and taken home to sleep; now we must load you up for sleep too."

Unci pulls me into her lap, wrapping a blanket around us. I lay my head against Unci's heart as I listen to the stories Lala and her share.

Unci is my favorite person. Sitting on her lap and listening to her tell stories is my favorite place to be.

A simple prayer starts,
with familiar words
floating through the air.

Hau mitakuyepi
Hello my relatives.

Iyuha cante wasteya nape ciyuzapi
With good feelings in my heart, I extend my hand to all of you.

Le anpetu kin lila waste
This is a really good day.

Anpetu kin le mni wiconi na makhoche kin naunzinpi kte!
Today we are going to stand for the water and land!

Ithusekas mni na makhoche kin awananglakapi kte.
At all costs, we will protect the water and land!

Mitakuye Oyasin
All my relations

Too soon night has fallen. The tipis are raised, the food has been eaten, and the stories have been told. My eyes feel heavy, but I am not ready for sleep.

"I want to stay . . ." I protest, trying to push the sleepy away.

Lala Miles lifts me into his strong embrace and Unci LaDonna rubs soft circles on my back.

"We need to go home and rest. Don't worry, we will be back tomorrow, and the next day and every day thereafter to fight the Black Snake. We will be here to defend as long as the Black Snake keeps attacking, my girl," Lala Miles assures me.

I look at the Sacred Stone Camp in the evening's dusky hues.
The land looks serene, a beacon of hope for the upcoming fight.

We are ready to protect the water and land. The Sacred Stone is where we make our stand.

On April 1, 2016, LaDonna BraveBull Allard, with the loving support of her husband, Miles Allard, alongside her family, her Standing Rock Lakota Nation, and the many other brave protectors who stood with her, took the courageous step forward, onto the world stage, to say enough is enough! The Sacred Stone Camp was built as a direct action against the desecration of important grave sites, sacred sites, and finite resources carelessly being demolished and/or endangered by Energy Transfer's Dakota Access Pipeline. Every one of LaDonna's actions, up to, during, and since DAPL's attack were taken to protect all life that depends on Unci Maka (Grandmother Earth). LaDonna loved the land and waters; she spent her life working to protect a future that includes clean waters, breathable air, and safe lands. LaDonna's spirit remains a testament to what you can do when you are motivated by love, inspired by good intentions, and bound with the courage to stand up for what is right. Even after LaDonna and Miles left their physical forms behind, their spirits remain, inspiring everyone who hears or knows their stories to do better, to be braver, and to be the best protectors of water and land that we can!

Left to right: the statue Not Afraid to Look designed & built by Charles Rencountre (Oceti Sakowin) which overlooks the Sacred Stone lands (Inyan Wakhánagapi Othí), a sacred stone, and LaDonna's final resting place which looks out onto the camp grounds

GLOSSARY

Unci (Uhn'chee) — Grandmother

Lala (La'La) — Grandfather

Tipi (Tee'Pee) — Home

Maka (Ma'Kah) — Earth

Left to right: LaDonna braiding her nephew Matt Remle's hair for his blanket wrapping ceremony and her two sons, Freedom and Will; LaDonna and Miles; LaDonna and the author, Rae Rose

For LaDonna —R.R.

For all of our relatives, human, animal, and nature. May we continue to care for and protect each other to create a beautiful Indigenous future. —A.M.

Dial Books for Young Readers
An imprint of Penguin Random House LLC
1745 Broadway, New York, New York 10019

First published in the United States of America by Dial Books for Young Readers, an imprint of Penguin Random House LLC, 2025

Text copyright © 2025 by Rae Rose   •   Illustrations copyright © 2025 by Aly McKnight

Visit us online at PenguinRandomHouse.com.

Library of Congress Cataloging-in-Publication Data is available.

ISBN 9780593696637   •   Manufactured in China   •   TOPL   •   10 9 8 7 6 5 4 3 2 1

This book was edited by Michelle Lee, copyedited and proofread by Regina Castillo, and designed by Cerise Steel.
The production was supervised by Jayne Ziemba, Nicole Kiser, Alisha Churma, and Caitlin Taylor..

Text set in Chella

The illustrator of this book created the art with watercolor and graphite on Arches 300 lb. watercolor paper.

Photos courtesy of the author.

The authorized representative in the EU for product safety and compliance is Penguin Random House Ireland,
Morrison Chambers, 32 Nassau Street, Dublin D02 YH68, Ireland, https://eu-contact.penguin.ie.